Surviving a Traumatic Parenthood

Surviving a Traumatic Parenthood

Tools to Use After Your Child is Arrested and Goes to Rehab

Susan Peticolas

Hideaway Press
645 Forest St
Reno, NV   89509
Email: support@survivingatraumaticparenthood.com
    orders@survivingatraumaticparenthood.com
    775-338-9192
Website: www.survivingatraumaticparenthood.com

ISBN-13 978-1456447694

Resilience is accepting your new reality, even if it's less good than the one you had before.

-Elizabeth Edwards

Contents

Preface and Acknowledgments   9

Suggestions for Parents   11

If This Is a Lifelong Journey, Let
Me Get Off Now!   13

You Have Done Your Best with
The Skills That You Have   15

Let Go of Right or Wrong Thinking   17

Steer Your Own Boat. Let Your
Child Steer His.   19

Staying in my Business   21

A Boundary Is a Gift You Give
Yourself   25

Sometimes the Best Reaction Is
No Reaction   27

Let Go of Expectations   29

Obsessing About Your Child Is
Not Caring   31

The Only Way Out of the Pain
Is Through It   33

Are My Beliefs Serving Me?   37

Make It Easy   41

Is It a Hand Up or Hand Out?   45

Objectivity   49

Change the Wording   51

Coping   55

A New Relationship with Your Son
or Daughter   57

Goals   61

Campfire Healing   63

Putting It All Together   65

Final Thoughts   73

Preface and Acknowledgments

When my son was arrested for the first time, he was sixteen. I sensed that this was a marker in our lives that would change our family forever. It took us down a path we had never been. At the time, I could find no comfort. I could not imagine how my life could go on if my son went to prison. I could not find the help I needed. I felt utterly and totally alone. It seemed that no one else was facing the same problems I was.

After several weeks I was leaving the jail after a visit, and another mother was entering the jail. It looked as if it was her first visit, and she was unsure of what to do. As she was going through the metal detector, I caught sight of her eyes, and I saw the same terror and sorrow that I had. I felt connected to her, and I wanted to reach out, but I had no words of comfort. I was empty, and I had nothing to give. This book is for her and for all the others that have had to, and will have to, go down this path of addiction and criminal behavior with someone you love and are powerless to change.

Use this book any way you want. Write in its margins, underline ideas you like and black out those you don't. Each chapter provides an idea and then an exercise to help shift your thinking. You can pick chapters at random, choose those that resonate with you most, or read it from start to finish. Do them in a parent support group, with a counselor, with a friend or by yourself. I hope the exercises spark ideas that move you towards healing.

I am not sure anyone writes alone. I think we are more connected than we realize. And although help was hard to find, it was there. I found help through a six week class The National Alliance on Mental Illness sponsored, through counselors, through the women in my support group, through Al-Anon, and Nar-Anon. I also have an understanding and

9

supportive partner and sister who have been there with insight and love.

This work is a thank you to all those people who helped me, and hopefully, a gift to all those parents who have or will need to find a way to take back their lives and find contentment again.

Suggestions for Parents

1. Do not take your son or daughter's behavior personally.

2. Even if your son or daughter never changes, when you change your behavior you can have a new and different relationship.

3. Obsessing about your child is not caring. It only robs you of your life.

4. Rescuing your child robs him of the consequences he has earned and the dignity to solve his own problems.

5. Let go of expectations.

6. Setting a boundary is a gift to you and to your child.

7. Sometimes the best reaction is no reaction.

8. Steer your own boat. Let your son or daughter steer his or hers.

9. You are more than a parent. Nurture yourself.

10. If you let go of controlling your child and the outcome of her actions, then all you have left to do is to love her.

If This Is a Lifelong Journey, Let Me Off Now!

My son had behavior issues from the time he could walk. When he was a toddler, I assured myself that once he mastered speech his behavior would improve. When he was a preschooler, I waited for the days of childhood to tame him. In the pre-teen years, I told myself it was a phase. His teenage years brought more chaos and defiance. I looked forward to him becoming an adult.

When he was sixteen, I found my way to a parent support group. I remember that first meeting. We sat in a circle and introduced ourselves. It was with startled amazement that I realized the age of the children that some of these parents were talking about. "I have a twenty-eight year old son who doesn't work." "I have a thirty-five year old daughter who is homeless." "I have a forty-seven year old son who lives with me."

I had never considered that this might be a lifelong journey, and that adulthood might not cure my son. I'd accepted responsibility for my son's behavior until he was eighteen, and I was looking forward to the day this responsibility ended. Now I was hearing stories of parents staying on this merry-go-round of accepting responsibility for someone else's behavior well into their retirement. That day I vowed that somehow I would find a way to live my own life and let my son live his.

I have heard that as baby eaglets are maturing the parent eagles stop feeding the eaglets. They tempt the eaglets by dropping food away from the nest. They make the nest smaller and less comfortable. Could nature help me design a plan for independence?

-What changes could your child make, so you could be happy?

-If your child never made these changes, could you still be happy?

-What brings you joy and happiness that does not involve your child?

-In what ways do you foster dependence in your adult child?

-In what ways do you foster independence in your adult child?

You Have Done Your Best with the Skills That You Have

One of the things that has brought me great pain is wondering if I could have or should have done something different. I wonder what I could have done to change the outcome of my son's life. I question if somehow I have caused his addiction. I wonder if I should have been stricter or more lenient. Would the outcome have been different if I had worked less, reacted more calmly, said or had not said different things?

I shared this with a counselor once, and she assured me I had done my best. But that did not make me feel better because I did not believe it. She then asked me to do an exercise that finally loosened the grip of my guilt. She asked me to write down everything I had done for my son. That week I sat down and wrote down everything. I wrote down what I had done for him as an infant, a toddler a pre-schooler, a child, and a teenager. I wrote down the involvement I had with his schools. I noted all the teachers I worked with, the principals I talked to, the counselors and doctors I employed. I mentioned the limits I set, the books I read, the time I spent with him. I wrote it all down, and I finally saw that I had done my best.

-On the next page, give yourself the opportunity to acknowledge that you have done your best. Make a list. Take your time in doing this, leaving nothing out. Allow yourself to release guilt. Allow yourself to know you have done your best.

-If you need help getting started consider the following questions:

-Before my child went to school, what did I do for him or her?

-Once my child went to school, what did I do for him or her?

15

-Did I seek help from professionals?

-Did I team with teachers and counselors?

-When my child became an adolescent, what did I try?

-Once my son or daughter was an adult how did I reach out to him or her to foster his or her growth?

Let Go of Right or Wrong Thinking

As a child I grew up in a Catholic family and went to a Catholic school. Almost every action was characterized as either right or wrong. I remember having conversations, and after I would finish talking, I was either given approval for what I had said or not. And although my family and my school were not really punitive, there was an underlying belief that wrongs would be righted.

Then I had my own children. My oldest son challenged me from the beginning. He was in trouble at school, he lied, he did not follow rules, and he did not seem to learn from consequences. For years I applied the black and white ideology in my head and probably in his too. And as experience has softened my outlook, I realize that my ability to love him has nothing to do with his "goodness" or "badness."

Finally I challenged this belief and realized that right or wrong thinking was not a belief that was serving me. It made me unhappy. When I learned that I could loosen the grip that right and wrong thinking had on me, I could see actions as neither good nor bad and consequences as neither right nor wrong. I can take the blame and shame out of my thinking.

-Write down some of your beliefs and examine whether they have right and wrong thinking in them. Here is an example of one of mine. "My son is a heroin addict. He has ruined his life and mine too. The only way for us to ever have happiness again is for him to stop."

-Some of my beliefs include:

-Rewrite your statement without blame or right and wrong thinking. I have given an example of how I changed mine. "My son is a heroin addict. I choose not to be involved in his addiction and to allow his consequences to occur. But I love him and will find ways to demonstrate my love that do not enable his addiction. My happiness is not dependent on him."

Steer Your Own Boat. Let Your Child Steer His.

I have a clear idea of what my drug addicted son needs to do to get out of his predicaments. I see that continuing on his path takes so much more energy than it would if he would follow the rules of society.

I also see that my trying to plan my son's life is futile and takes so much more of my energy than if I were to allow him to live his own life. My worry is counterproductive and produces no results. If I drop the obsession about how my son lives his life, my life becomes lighter, calmer, and easier.

Think of two kayaks on a river. You are in one and your adult child is in another. Your child ventures ahead looking for excitement. You shout out warnings about rocks, rapids and whirlpools. He continues on and gets farther from your sights. You kneel to shout to him, sure that he is in trouble. Suddenly you realize that while you had the illusion that you were guiding your child in his kayak, your boat has approached rapids and is quickly headed to a waterfall.

-How do you shout directions to your child?

-If you steered only your own boat, where would you steer it?

-Where do you want to go?

-Who do you want to be?

-What do you want to experience?

-What do you want to accomplish?

Staying In My Business.

Much of my pain comes from wanting my children to behave differently or to strive for goals that are important to me. When I dream that my son will save money or choose a career that will bring him what I consider to be a good income, I am basing what he should do on what is important to me. Often these dreams become an obsession, and I begin to manipulate, cajole and push my son to do what will make me feel safe and happy. When I rely on someone else's actions to fulfill my hopes and dreams, I have given up my own power.

One way out of the pain is to look at whose business I am in. I define my business as anything affecting me directly and their business as everything else. I've heard it described as concretely as to imagine a hula-hoop around your body. Your business is that which falls within the hula-hoop.

-For practice label the following "M" for "my business" and "T" for "their business".

_____My son should get a full time job.

_____My daughter should save at least $100.00 a month.

_____I should get more exercise.

_____If I could get my son to attend a recovery meeting he might find people who would foster his sobriety.

_____She wastes so much time on the computer.

_____If my daughter would tell me the truth, I would trust her.

-Now rewrite all the thoughts above that were "their business" and rephrase them to make it "my business." So "My son should get a full time job" becomes "I should have a full time job." "My daughter should save at least $100.00 a month" is re-written "I should save $100.00 a month."

-Make a list of the thoughts in your head. Include the things you think you or other people should do.

-Label them M for "my business" and T for "their business."

Rewrite the thoughts that are "their business" and make them "my business."

A Boundary is a Gift I Give to Myself and the Other Person

My son's problems and his urgency about them seem to escalate as the sun goes down, and it gets closer to my bedtime. His most urgent calls are at midnight or later. The later it becomes the more demanding he is, turning his emergency into my urgency.

If he calls me crying, begging or yelling, I don't give in. I know that if I do, it strengthens his desire to call me to solve his problems. But I am awakened, and when I hang up the phone, I don't doze quickly back to sleep. Instead I toss and turn, worry and obsess, and feel drained in the morning.

Finally I made a decision. I told my son I would not accept any phone calls from him after 6:00 p.m. I told him that I was not able to get back to sleep after I talked to him, so I was exhausted the next day. I went further and decided to turn the phone off when I went to bed, so I wouldn't be awakened by the ringing of the phone.

Although I've heard that this is an application of "tough love," I think it is different. Tough love by definition is used when someone treats another person harshly or sternly with the intent to help him in the long run. Setting a boundary based on my needs, is different than tough love to produce a result in another person. When I set a boundary that is about taking care of myself without blame or shame, it is less inflammatory and more loving. When I set a boundary, I give a gift to the other person. I outline for them what I need in our relationship to feel safe. As a result I am more open and not resentful.

-List an action that your son or daughter does that brings you pain.

-What boundary could you set that focuses on your need to care for yourself rather than your desire to change your child's behavior?

Sometimes the Best Reaction Is No Reaction

I have learned that the drug addict often redirects attention from himself by making accusations towards me. I know I am in trouble when my son starts listing my faults to deflect my attention off of him. And when I take the bait it is like anteing up at a poker game. I begin to argue, to build my case, to defend my actions. When I put my ante in, the poker game begins, and the craziness escalates.

When this happens, there is never a winner. I've never had my son meekly agree that I am right. I've learned that once the craziness escalates, it is time to retreat. It is okay for me not to defend myself. It is okay to say nothing and walk away or hang up the phone. I need to push myself away from the poker table and let him know I no longer play this kind of game. Nothing is accomplished with arguing with a using drug addict. The drug addict is not the person I know and love. I am not arguing with my son but with my son on drugs. I will never win.

-Describe a situation where you and your child got in a heated argument.

-At what point could you have walked away to prevent the escalation of the argument?

-Here is a list of ways to disengage and some comments that do not escalate behavior. Circle the ones that you are willing to try and add some of your own.

ACTION	COMMENT
Walk away.	-There are many ways to look at it.
Drive off.	-I will get back to you.
Go to the bathroom.	-I need to think about that.
Mow the lawn .	-Now I know how you feel.
Use the leaf blower.	-I don't have the answer.
Go to the grocery store.	-I'm sorry you feel like that.
Roll up the window.	-You may be right.
Call a friend.	

Let Go of Expectations

Anthropologist and author Angeles Arrien cites four rules for a happy life. They are:
1. Show up.
2. Pay attention.
3. Tell the truth.
4. Don't be attached to the results.

The first three are sometimes hard but seem possible. That last one about letting go of the results is the hard one. We have attachments and expectations all the time. We have them for ourselves, our co-workers, our spouses, our friends, and of course our children. When my children were young, I had expectations that my sons would do well in school, have good friends, graduate from high school, and go to college. I envisioned prom and high school graduation and family dinners.

However my expectations did not come to fruition. In fact, my troubled son stole bikes, did graffiti, got in fights, got involved in gangs, and finally went to prison. I remember sharing with a friend that I just wanted my son to have peace. She pointed out that maybe that was what I wanted, but it certainly didn't look like that was what he wanted. A short time after that my son and I were texting, and I said something to the effect that I wanted peace for him, and he texted back, "Sorry mom, I love chaos."

So I can attach myself to the results and maintain my expectations for him, but they likely will bring me disappointment. If I realign my expectations and let go of the results, I can realign my life to be about me.

-Write down your expectations of your children. Include accomplishments, holidays and family gatherings.

-Consider that these are not your child's expectations of himself. If you released yourself from these expectations or attachments, what would your life look like?

-What expectations do you think your parent(s) or family had of you?

-Which ones did you meet, and which ones didn't you meet and why?

Obsessing About Your Child Is Not Caring. It Only Robs You Of Your Life.

I am a visiting nurse, and years ago when my kids were small children, I remember a visit I made. I drove up to my patient's home just as the mail carrier was placing her mail in the mailbox. I took the mail from the carrier and brought it in to my patient. On top of the pile was a letter from the state prison. When I handed it to my patient, she said, "Oh there's a letter from my son." My heart opened up with compassion, and I thought to myself, "I would die if one of my sons went to prison."

Several years later my son was sentenced to a six month military style boot camp, which was part of the state prison system. I was devastated and couldn't imagine how I was going to make it through his six months. I conjured up thoughts of people abusing him, belittling him, and even beating him. I went so far as to do a search on the internet of the specific camp to which he was sent. There I found an article from a mother stating that it is unbelievable that these forms of punishment exist in our society. I hurt for my son. I suffered with him. I imagined myself there and wondered how I would make it through.

When he came home he looked better than he had looked for years. His eyes were bright, his skin flawless and his body in magnificent shape. He was on fire with the physical gains he had made. He told me at length about the obstacle courses, the runs and the hikes. He had such pride in his accomplishments.

My six months of hell imagining what he was going through were a total waste of time. It produced nothing but misery for me. My projection that he would react as I would in the same situation was totally inaccurate. My bottom is not his bottom, and it serves no purpose for me to pick up his consequences and worry about them.

31

-What are your greatest fears about your child and his addiction?

-When you play these fears out in your head, how does it help your child or you?

-Each time you begin to worry about your child go to your journal and write about it. What happened for me is I saw that I was worrying and obsessing about the same thing over and over again. My worry did not solve a problem but rather only perpetuated the circle of obsession.

-What would your life be like if you put down the worry about his consequences?

The Only Way Out of the Pain is Through It

Sometimes it's hard to deal with feelings until we know what the feeling is. It can be a hard task to identify our emotions and our grief. But when we identify them and accept them, we begin a step in healing. Writing can help us identify our feelings. Poetry templates can often be helpful in getting those emotions identified and out on paper. The purpose of this exercise is to express our feelings, and the poem itself is not important. We are trying to identify our emotions, so we can move through them. Here are three examples of poetry templates. Choose one.

Write an Instant Poem

Think of the book you most loved to read to your child. Imagine your child tired from a long day. He or she has just gotten out of the bath and is ready for bed. You grab your favorite book to read to him. What is it?

After you identify the book, write the title. Use each of the words as the beginning of a new line. Suppose your favorite book was Cloudy With a Chance of Meatballs. Each word will begin a new line.

Cloudy days ahead,

With rain pouring, and I not understanding why…

A bucket of hopes and dreams dashed and a

Chance of my dreams crashing to an end.

Of all the possibilities I thought this life might contain

Meatballs was not what I thought I'd end up with…

33

Here's another poetry template:

I'm the type of parent who always looked for_____

_____

Who always saw_____

_____

Who always wanted_____

_____

Who always got_____

_____

I'm the type of parent who never looked for_____

_____

Who never saw_____

_____

Who never wanted _____

_____

Who never got_____

_____

But today I'm the type of parent who looks_____

_____

Who sees_____

_____

Who wants_____

_____

Who gets_____

_____

And another one:

The Bio Poem

My name is _____

I am (list three character traits)_____

_____

I am related to (list close family members)_____

_____

I like (list three things you like)_____

_____

I love (list three things you love)_____

_____

I wish (list three things you wish)_____

_____

_

I admire (list three things you admire)_____

_____

I need (list three things you need)_____

_____

I aspire to (list three things you aspire to)_____

_____

Are My Beliefs Serving Me?

A belief is something we tell ourselves over and over. We gather beliefs from an earlier time. Many of our beliefs come from our family of origin or from a religion that we were raised with. We strengthen these beliefs by telling ourselves the same story over and over again. Many of our beliefs serve us well and help us to function productively in society. I believe saving money each month will help me in retirement.

But some beliefs can foster guilt, a sense of failure, or even depression. Because we believe that the way we see the world is accurate, we don't challenge those beliefs. But not all of our stories serve us. I had some beliefs about parenthood, education, and children that were sabotaging my life. My sabotaging beliefs included:

1. Any child if given love and the right kind of structure can succeed.
2. Nurture is far more important than nature. If parents are good enough they will have good children.
3. Children who succeed at school will succeed at life.
4. People in prison are bad people.

Because of these beliefs, when my children weren't doing well in school, when they didn't get good grades, when they had difficulty in school, and when finally one of them went to prison, I took on guilt for those actions and saw myself as a failure. With some help I decided to challenge my beliefs and to begin to change the stories I repeated over and over again.

-Look at the belief: **"Nurture is far more important than nature. If parents are good enough they will have**

successful children." If that is true, then the following is also true:

-Successful children always have good parents.
-Unsuccessful children have bad parents.
-Bad parents never have successful children.
-Parents determine how successful children will be.
-Children's successes are determined by parents.

This black and white thinking is challenged when we re-word the belief. We can begin to chip away at these ingrained beliefs.

-Look at my belief: **"People in prison came from bad homes."** If this is true, what is also true? Practice by turning the belief around.

-What are some of your beliefs about child-rearing?

-Are there any beliefs you have that cause you to feel guilty?

-What are some of your beliefs about good and bad behavior?

-Turn these beliefs around to see if they are valid. Consider that challenging some of your beliefs may set you free.

Make It Easy

The other day I closed the front door to my home, and the handle simply fell off in my hand. As I stood there with my mouth wide open staring at the handle, I figured out that it probably had been working continuously for around forty years.

After I returned from the hardware store with a new handle, I spread the directions out and got all my tools ready. I got the handle almost on, and then it didn't quite fit, so I was tempted to force it into place. But I have a wise friend who told me that forcing repairs is a mistake. She told me that her husband (who is a builder) says if he forces anything, it is a sure thing that it will not work with ease. And when he feels the need to force something he backs off and only starts again when he can do it without force. I took the advice, backed off, and started over. The handle and lock now worked with complete ease.

I then thought about how to apply this to my son. When he tells me he is ready for a new start, I let my heart jump for joy. I start planning how I can help him, think about what he needs to do, give gentle reminders, and offer rides. Everything is there for him, and I find myself pushing, maneuvering and manipulating him into doing what will make me happy. But usually, despite his words, I can't quite get him to complete things as I would. I become frustrated. I get that same feeling of wanting to push or cajole him into action that I got when I was trying to push or force the lock into place. I become frustrated and angry. I can offer help once, but when I continually offer help or advice I have moved out of being helpful and into pushing and forcing a solution.

I'm learning that if something seems really difficult, perhaps that is because it's not going to fall into place and work with ease. I turn down the volume of my son's voice and look at his actions. There is no need to put a lot of energy into what my son tells me because it is his life and his goals. My role is to love him, not to be the action in his life. If he asks for help, I can provide it if I want, and if it can be done with ease. Otherwise it won't work out anyway.

-Describe a time that you tried to help your son or daughter when the outcome did not turn out as you had hoped. Describe the incident by first telling what you hoped the end result would be. Then describe what you did to help or to force. And lastly describe how things turned out.

 I hoped the end result would be:

What I did to help was:

The end result was:

-Can you see where things became difficult and when you were forcing solutions?

-When did you begin to repeat yourself?

-Share what you wrote with someone who is not closely involved, and see if they have the same or a different perspective.

Is it a Hand Up or Hand Out?

People can and do change their lives. Kids are people and people make mistakes. It's not unusual for parents to help their kids out when they get in a bind. We are compassionate with our children, and our hearts open and we want to help them. We are hardwired to help our children. We want them to have a good life. But if the hand we extend to help them is met time and time again with requests for more assistance, then it is no longer a hand up but just simply a hand out.

I want you to read about a scenario with my son. Try to see when things started to unravel. Try to differentiate between that which was done with ease and that which became difficult. See if you can see when the hand up became a hand out.

My twenty-one year old son had been released from prison and was staying with his father. While in prison we had discussed an outpatient treatment center for heroin addiction. He had heard good reviews of it and thought it was his best chance of recovery. I called and was pleased to find out that I could afford to pay for the program. The day after he was released I went with him and met the staff and paid for a month of treatment. I purchased a bus pass, so he could make it to his appointments. He is very artistic and shared that he wanted to become a tattoo artist. I have some money that I had saved for college, and I told him if he put together a list of equipment and prices, I'd consider purchasing the equipment. I bought him pens and paper, so he could work on his drawings.

A week or two later he shared with me that he had a tremendous desire to use. He talked with his counselor, and they made an appointment with the physician on staff for possible prescription medication to help with the urges. He had to be at the center at 6:30 a.m., and since there was no

45

bus at that hour, I agreed to pick him up. I asked him to call me when he woke up, so I'd know he was ready. When I looked at the clock that morning and it was 6:00, I called him. He sounded sleepy but said he'd be ready. After the doctor's appointment he slept in the car and was irritable.

The physician had not had enough time to do a complete assessment so had requested he return in several days. This time when I arrived to pick him up he was in the shower. After his shower he poured himself some cereal and milk, so he could have some breakfast. He was irritable and assured me he did not have to be on time.

Several days later I asked about the tattooing. He said he needed about $700.00 to get started but hadn't had the time to look online to get a list of supplies because he didn't have access to a computer. I suggested the public library, but he said the wait was too long. I suggested my office, but he said he didn't want to have to wait for a ride home after he used the computer.
Several more days later I discovered he was using again.

It's hard to pinpoint when things actually started to become hard. That is real life. Things aren't black and white. There is not one moment but rather a gradual change. When you read the scenario what are some of the red flags you see that indicate that I was no longer giving a hand up but a hand out?

-Allow yourself to describe a recent incident with your son or daughter where you offered to do something for them that did not turn out as you had planned?

-Can you see where you stopped giving a hand up and started giving a hand out?

-Were you working harder than your son or daughter?

-Is there anything you did for your son or daughter that he or she could have done for himself or herself?

Objectivity

One of the greatest gifts that has brought me healing is to have been able to be part of groups where I could listen to other parents describe what was happening with their kids. As a member I only listened; no advice was given. That way when I listened to their stories, I wasn't thinking and preparing what I was going to say in response, but I truly listened. The gift was that I could see the manipulation, exploitation, and dysfunction in other people's stories. I could see it when looking from an objective point of view. But because I am involved in my own story, it is not as clear. It is easier to see what is happening when you can see it from the outside.

-Write a scenario of your story (or use one that you have outlined before). Read it aloud and see if you can see the disease or the point where the direction seemed to change, and you were giving hand outs. When did the effort of your relationship become so great?

-Re-write the same scenario, but change the names and pronouns so that it is as if you are talking about someone else. Read it aloud again and see if it changes your viewpoint at all.

-Read it to someone else using the changed names and pronouns and see if it changes their perspective.

Change the Wording

One of my biggest challenges is releasing the guilt I sometimes feel for the predicament that my son is in. I wonder if I'd done something differently if the outcome would be different. During those times I find that my self talk can tell only one side of the story. "Maybe if I'd gotten him help earlier, he would not have gone down the dark path of drugs." But I leave out the part that I was there with him, seeking help from teachers, counselors, and doctors. I leave out the part of how hard I tried. I have found that one way I'm able to let go of the guilt and anguish my child's behavior causes me is to change the wording of my thoughts.

I was talking to a friend, and she said she felt guilty for kicking her son out of the house. I asked her to step back and look at the broader picture. Before she kicked her son out, he became so angry at her that he put holes in the wall and threatened her. If she said she felt guilty for kicking her son out, she was only reviewing half the story.

When I think of my son, I sometimes see him on a roller coaster riding in the first seat, while I am holding on with my fingertips, and my body is flapping in the wind. The rollercoaster is zooming along the track at frightening speeds, taking turns where only one wheel is left on the track, entering multiple looptey loops, and taking nose dives at breakneck speeds. All the while my son is laughing with glee, hands raised overhead. I on the other hand, release one of my two hands (that are gripping earnestly) to push him back in the cart, as my body is slapped back and forth in the wind.

I can still be a parent, but I can relinquish the role of back seat driver in his life. I can let go of the anguish of his decisions and allow him his own consequences. I can still love him and care for him without assuming responsibility for him. I can change my wording of my self talk when I feel guilty for his actions and the predicaments they put him in.

Experience tells me that the wording I use can influence my feelings. I can tell myself "*I deserted my daughter in her darkest hour.*" Or I can re-word the thought, "*She was unaware of the hold drugs had on her life, and my rescuing her out of jail isn't going to help her.*"

Here are some other examples:

"*I refused to let my son get his drivers license.*"
becomes:
"*My son has not kept a 2.0 grade point average so he hasn't gotten his license.*"

"*I let my daughter sit in jail.*"
becomes:
"*My daughter chose to drive while under the influence and now is suffering the consequences.*"

"*I refused to let my daughter go on her senior trip.*"
becomes:
"*My daughter and I agreed to share the expenses of her senior trip. She did not earn her share of the fare, so she isn't going.*"

Try re-wording the following statements:

"*I refuse to let my son drive my car.*" (His car finally stopped running because of multiple fender-benders.)

52

"I kicked my son out." (He pawned your big screen t.v)

"I've refused to let my daughter go on our vacation this summer." (She cut so many classes she did not get credit for her last semester and needs to go to summer school.)

"I *refuse to let my son use my computer"* (You got a nasty virus when he downloaded porn.)

Coping

Having a child delve into the world of drugs is a mind boggling, gut wrenching, fall-on-your-knees kind of experience for a parent. It seems too big to tackle. But every day the sun rises again, and, although we wish when we open our eyes in our first alertness from sleep that this addiction was a dream, it is not. Each new day we tackle our new reality. Our child is a drug addict.

Thinking about this fact is a daily, hourly, and even minute-by-minute affair. Our relationships with a spouse, other children, parents and co-workers suffer because so much of our energy is spent thinking about and helping this addicted child. I find myself rehashing our last encounter or obsessing about where he is right now. Doing this robs me of my life.

Unfortunately many of us will find that our children do not come out of addiction for a long time. It serves us to learn how to function with this reality and how to give our time and attention to other relationships and activities. I have found several activities that have helped me cope.

I imagine that I have 100 units of energy a day. Some days I find I use 99 of them on worrying or thinking about my son who is not here, and over whom I have no control. Those are not good days. So I decide to dole out my units of energy differently. I dole out a hefty dose to work. I dole another dose to my son who is here with me and not addicted. I dole out a dose to my partner and throw some in for a friend. I dole some out to myself to do something fun with myself. I try to see that giving my addicted son an unequal portion of my energy helps no one. I am his parent, but I am much more than that, just as he is much more than my son.

I also find it helpful to shift from the small picture to the big picture. I picture my son. I picture the room he is in and what he is doing in the room. I send him love. I then

55

remove myself from the room and picture him from outside looking through the window. Then I back myself farther away as if I am in a tree, and I see the building he is in, the window of his room and him inside the room. I send him and everyone else in the building love. I back up again, and I see the whole neighborhood and the streets, and the building and the room. I send love like rays of the sun. I continue backing up for as long as I need.

Another means of coping I find helpful is to construct an imaginary container. My container is a very large storage shed. (My son's problems are very large!) Throughout the day, when images of him come up, I imagine that I put anything to do with his problems into the storage shed to be dealt with when I have time to sort through it all. I tell myself I have other things to attend to right now, and, for the sake of sanity, I will need to store those thoughts.

My last coping mechanism involves developing a safe place to go. I have developed a place for myself where I can be alone, peaceful and content. If I am trying to sleep and keep thinking about my son, I try to soothe myself by returning to this place where I know I am safe. There is a path I walk down that is remote. I walk for quite awhile until I can see the ocean and a beautiful beach. There is one chair at the beach. The sun is setting, and the air around me is perfect. I sit on the chair which reclines back. I close my eyes. I can hear the surf. I feel a gentle wind on my face and I can smell and taste the salt in the air.

-Of the four examples which ones would work best for you?

-Describe other coping mechanisms that work for you.

Even If Your Son or Daughter Never Changes, When You Change Your Behavior You Can Have a New and Different Relationship

Assume that 1 is you, 2 is your drug addicted son and 3 is your relationship. 1=your part in the relationship, 2=your son's part in the relationship, and 3=the sum total of your and your son's relationship.

Suppose you change your part in the relationship and label that 4. Since you have no power over changing your son you will continue to label his part in the relationship as 2. But when you change your part of the relationship, the equation now becomes $4+2 = 6$. So the relationship becomes completely different even if your drug addicted son never changes anything.

What could you change in your relationship with your son or daughter? Here is a hypothetical example.

I expect my son to get a job. I get daily job alerts for the types of jobs I think he could get and that he would enjoy. I then call him or text him with the information and eagerly wait for him to respond. (Let's label this 1.)

Next there is no response from my son. If I'm lucky enough to catch him and ask him about his follow through, he is evasive and tells me thanks, and he's looking into it. (Let's label this 2.)

I feel irritated. I suspect that he didn't follow through, and I'm angry because I feel suspicious. I feel worried. I call him again and leave a long voice mail about my feelings and tell him I'm irritated, angry, suspicious and worried. I don't hear back from him. The perfect job alert shows up in my e-mail. I decide to apply for him since I know this job would suit him so well. (Let's label this 3.)

1+2=3

I'll change my attitude and see how this works.

I acknowledge this is not working. I may want my son to get a job, but who knows if that will happen. I decide that I will not talk to my son about a job for a month. I text him and say good morning but nothing else. I decide that I will take a yoga class twice a week and go to the library and get a book on Italian cooking. (We'll label this 4.)

There is no response from my son. (We'll label this 2.)

I'm enjoying yoga and make some great pasta dishes. I still think about my son and send him loving wishes and occasional text. I'm not sure what the future holds for my son, but I know that my life feels more serene.
4+2=6

-Think about your relationship with your son or daughter. Can you describe a pattern and label it 1+2=3.

1=my part

2=his part

3=our relationship

`Think of ways you could change 1, to give yourself a new relationship with your son or daughter.

Goals

We all have a picture of what we'd like our lives to look like. We all have hopes and dreams. From the time we were young the picture has probably changed, and, depending on the day or year, our goals may be different. But just for today list your goals. They can be small or big.

1.

2.

3.

4.

5.

6.

7.

8.

After writing down the goals, look at each one carefully and decide if this is a goal you can achieve through your own action, or if it is dependent on another person. Some of your goals may center around your children as mine did. One of my goals was that my son would graduate from high school and college. It is perfectly normal for me to want my children to graduate from high school and college, but these are hopes for them and are not goals that I can achieve. These goals are dependent on another person's actions so they might be my son's goals (or not), but they are not goals that are achievable by my own effort. If we can differentiate between what is and isn't within our reach, we can save ourselves a lot of pain

Campfire Healing

You are a parent. But you are more than a parent. You are a multi-dimensional person who happens to be a parent. When tragedies occur with children, your sorrow can skew your vision of yourself. The following exercise will help you see yourself as a more complete whole person.

You are out in the woods. It is evening and the moon peeks out brightly from clouds that pillow the sky. You put on a light jacket and grab your flashlight and begin the short stroll to the campfire. The air is nippy, and, as you approach you can hear others talking with laughter interlaced between conversations. You can smell the campfire, and, as you approach you feel the warmth emanating from the fire itself. Marshmallows are already being roasted. There are ten chairs circling the campfire and one is not taken. That chair is for you. You are pleased to be here as you have wanted each and every person that is there to be sitting with you. You have invited them all. When you made up the invitation list you were told that you could invite anyone. You could invite family members, friends, someone who had died, a person from history, a pet, a fictional character, someone you greatly admire, someone you might want to get advice from, someone who comforts you…anyone. Look around and write down the names of the individuals you invited.

-Write down the names of the nine individuals you invited:

1.

2.

3.

4.

5.

6.

7.

8.

9.

-Look back at each individual and now write down next to their name what it is about that particular individual that made you invite him or her. What do you admire about them?

-Each and every quality you admire and saw in another person you possess yourself. You could not see the quality if you did not already have that within you. Write down these qualities on a card and keep them with you.

Putting It All Together

What we do for our children, we do because we love them. There is no other relationship where one member sacrifices so much for the benefit of the other. As parents we are hardwired to care for our children. But addiction changes the relationship, and the help we provide can actually perpetuate the problem. Following are the summary of conversations I had with three individuals who found recovery from their addiction.

"I'm a thirty-eight year old man, and I am a drug addict and alcoholic. I am proud of where I am today and how far I have come. But I work daily to let go of the guilt of who I was. I was an ungrateful and self centered teenager, which I guess is not that unusual. But I took things too far. I lived with my parents until I was twenty-seven. When I was twenty-four my parents told me I needed to pay $100.00 a month to go towards the utility bill. I was furious! I was not going to pay for my parents' utility bills. Never mind that I was barely working and spent the majority of my day satisfying my need for drugs and drink. I did not pay rent and freely ate any food that I wanted. I grudgingly agreed to pay the $100.00 but rarely actually gave my parents any money. Eventually they stopped asking. I guess I'm still ungrateful to some extent, because looking back I don't think my parents did me any favors by accepting my unacceptable behavior. Their helping me certainly did not prepare me for independence."

"I am a twenty-seven year old girl who has a twin brother and a younger sister who is twenty-five. I have a wonderful family, and they mean everything to me. I am not like my sister and brother. They always did well in school, went on to college, and moved out to live independently. I graduated from high school but never wanted to leave home. I'm not the type of person who likes to do things alone, and my parents understand that. I worked in retail businesses after high school and saved my money. I didn't want to move out

65

because I didn't want to spend my money. My addictions gradually got worse. It started with drinking too much, and taking xanax for my anxiety. Then it moved into harder drugs and black outs that ended in hospitalizations. I would drink and drug myself into oblivion. I lost lots of jobs and ended up going to jail and court ordered drug rehab. After my third DUI, I spent some time in prison. I am so sorry for the pain I have caused my family, and they mean the world to me. I can't imagine where I would have gone if they hadn't helped me and let me live with them. But I can say that what they did allowed me to continue using and drinking."

"I am a forty-nine year old woman and I did not find recovery from drug and alcohol abuse until I was thirty-five. When I was sixteen, my father, who was a policeman, killed himself. I had already begun to abuse alcohol and drugs before, but his death created a bigger hole that I tried to fill. One night I was loaded and driving, and I was stopped for a sobriety test. I flunked the test, but the police officer recognized me, and knowing that my father had killed himself, took pity on me. Instead of arresting me, he helped me in his car and gave me a lift home. I was thankful and knew I had dodged a bullet. What followed in my life was years of rebellion, unmet potential, and regrets from more than a decade and a half of drug abuse. Looking back, I have wondered how different my life might have been if I'd suffered the consequences of my behavior that first time I was pulled over."

At some point I started to see that my helping my son didn't serve me and wasn't helping him either. Once I challenged my beliefs and gathered strength, I was ready to set boundaries. I knew I was seeking a more serene life, and, through boundaries I was able to start.

A boundary is something we set to keep ourselves safe and to protect our serenity. A boundary is not set in hopes of changing another person. If we set it based on our own needs, it provides clarity to ourselves and to those around us. A boundary outlines to ourselves and to others what we want in our lives. When we set a boundary, we give a gift to both ourselves and those around us. We feel safe, and those around us know what we want and expect. When we have boundaries, we have less anger and resentment, and we open the door to more serenity and contentment.

When we set a boundary, how we do it is up to us. We don't have to announce it to the other person, or we can. We do not have to set the boundary in stone, or we can. When my son is not doing drugs, my boundaries are different than when he is doing drugs. I imagine boundaries to be like my car. When I am inside my car, I am in control of what happens. If I see someone I know, I can roll the windows down. If I don't like what's going on, I can raise the windows and lock the doors. I can stay parked with my windows up or I can drive away. Boundaries give us that same protection.

Think about what you want your relationship to look like with your son or daughter. What is it that you will and won't accept? What brings you pain, and what brings you joy? I find it helpful when setting boundaries to write down what I will not accept first. Then I think about what I am willing to do, and what I want our relationship to look like.

-Write down the behaviors you will not accept. (If you need suggestions, go to the next page and look at some I have used for myself.)

Some examples of what I will not do:

When you are using drugs, I do not want to be around you.

When we are talking, if there is yelling or profanity, I will leave.

I will not lend you my car.

You can not live with me.

I will not give you cash.

I will not lie for you.

I will not bail you out of jail.

I will not visit you in jail.

I will not pay your rent.

I will not accept calls after 6:00 p.m.

I need to have you call before coming over.

-Now make a list of those things that you will do. If you need suggestions look at some of the ones I've used on the next page.

Some examples of what I will do:

When you are sober, I will listen to you.

I will not offer advice unless you ask for it.

I will plan activities to do with you. (ping-pong, movies, cards)

I will take you to lunch on Sundays.

I will buy you a bus pass, and groceries and clothes.

I will write you letters in jail.

When we are scheduled to do something together I will have alternate plans, so, if you do not show up I am less disappointed.

I will pay for counseling.

I will pay for outpatient drug rehab.

I will go with you to doctor's appointments.

I will tell you that I love you.

Final Thoughts

Being a parent is hard work. But with tools and support you can find contentment whether or not your son or daughter finds sobriety. It doesn't come easily. Just when you think you've got it down you realize you don't. You stay in your own business until you realize you're in theirs. You don't have expectations until you do. You don't see things in black in white until there you are. You let go of old beliefs until they creep back in. But the difference is; now you have a different perspective and new goals. I'll end with something a dear friend once told me, "It's all up and down from here."

7331894R0

Made in the USA
Charleston, SC
18 February 2011